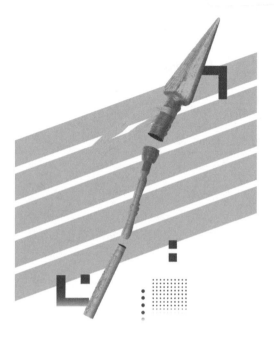

CHARACTERS

A ONE-YEAR EXPLORATION OF THE BIBLE THROUGH THE LIVES OF ITS PEOPLE

VOLUME THREE

THE KINGS

LifeWay Press • Nashville, Tennessee

Editorial Team, Student Ministry Publishing

Ben Trueblood
Director, Student Ministry

John Paul Basham
Manager, Student
Ministry Publishing

Drew Dixon
Editorial Team Leader,
Content Editor

Jesse Campbell
Content Editor

April-Lyn Caouette
Production Editor

Matt Atkinson
Art Director

Kaitlin Redmond
Graphic Designer

Published by LifeWay Press®
© 2020 LifeWay Press

No part of this work may be reproduced or transmitted in any form or by any means, electronic or mechanical, including photocopying and recording, or by any information storage or retrieval system, except as may be expressly permitted in writing by the publisher.

Requests for permission should be addressed in writing to LifeWay Press®, One LifeWay Plaza, Nashville, TN 37234-0144.

ISBN: 978-1-0877-0049-6
Item Number: 005823654

Dewey Decimal Classification Number: 242.2
Subject Heading: DEVOTIONAL LITERATURE / BIBLE STUDY AND TEACHING / GOD

Printed in the United States of America

Student Ministry Publishing
LifeWay Resources
One LifeWay Plaza
Nashville, TN 37234-0144

contents

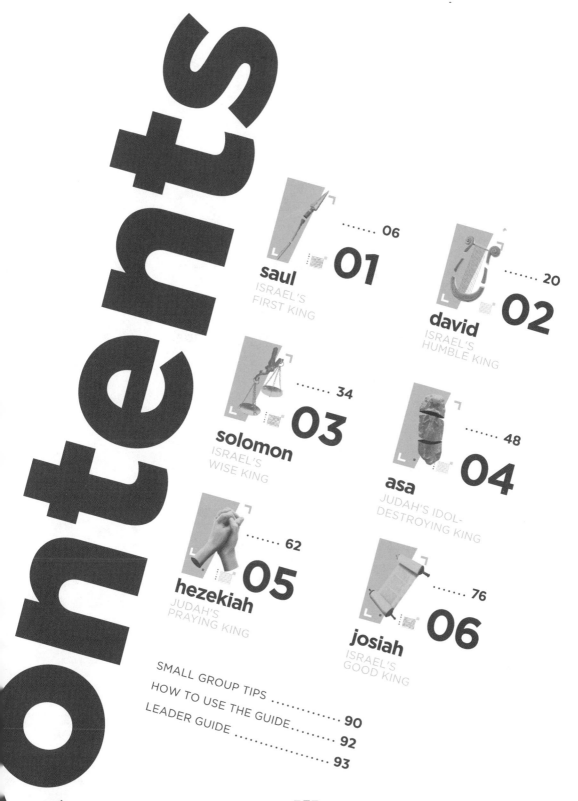

About Explore The Bible Students

The Whole Truth, For the Whole Student

When it comes to teens, don't avoid the truth. Don't sugarcoat it. *Explore the Bible: Students* helps you present teens with God's Word, allowing for honest and transparent conversations around the Bible as students learn how these ancient words speak into their lives today.

To find out more, go to **goExploreTheBible.com.**

How To Use This Study

This Bible study book includes six sessions of content for group and personal study. Regardless of what day of the week your group meets, each session begins with group study. Each group session utilizes the following elements to facilitate simple yet meaningful interaction among students.

INTRODUCTION
This page includes introductory content and questions to get the conversation started each time your group meets.

GROUP DISCUSSION
Continue the group discussion by reading the Scripture passages and discussing the questions on these pages. Finally, conclude each group session with a time of prayer, reflecting on what you have discussed.

BIOGRAPHY
This section provides more in-depth information regarding the biblical character being spotlighted each week and can be included in the group discussion or personal study times.

PERSONAL STUDY
Three personal studies are provided for each session to take students deeper into Scripture and to supplement the content introduced in the group study. With biblical teaching and personal questions, these sections help students grow in their understanding of God's Word and respond in faith.

LEADER GUIDE
A front-and-back Leader Guide for each session is provided on pages 93-104. It can be torn out to use in leading a group. It includes sample answers or discussion prompts to help you jump-start or steer the conversation.

01

introduction

When has doing things against God's way ever worked out?

God had created a nation through Israel from the slaves of Egypt. He delivered them from slavery through miraculous plagues that proved the Egyptian gods powerless, fed them as they traversed the desert under the leadership of Moses, and led them to the promised land under the leadership of Joshua.

When the people of God compared themselves to other nations, they realized a major difference: God's people had no earthly king to rule them. So they cried out for one. This was a rejection of their heavenly King, who had freed them from slavery and provided for them in the exodus from Egypt.

God allowed the people to have what they wanted, and through the prophet Samuel, an earthly king was chosen. Saul, Israel's first king, would not prove to be a perfect king. King Saul disobeyed God and insisted on his own way. This never works out well. God then had someone else anointed to succeed Saul to the throne, which enraged Saul.

When have you pushed back against the rules that were put over you?

Who is God to you? Why does obeying God matter?

ISRAEL'S FIRST KING
saul

Samuel said to Saul, "You have been foolish.
You have not kept the command the LORD your God
gave you. It was at this time that the LORD would have
permanently established your reign over Israel, but now
your reign will not endure."

1 SAMUEL 13:13-14

MONUMENT FOR HIMSELF

GROUP DISCUSSION

(get started)

focus attention

Do you think of yourself as a detail-oriented person?
Why is it important to pay attention to details even
though it might not come naturally to us?

**BETTER THAN
SACRIFICE**

explore the text

AS A GROUP, READ 1 SAMUEL 13:1, 5-14. ✳ ✎

01 . In what specific ways did Saul disobey God in these verses, and why was his disobedience so serious? In what ways can fear prompt people to disobey God?

02 . Was Saul's punishment too severe? Why or why not?

AS A GROUP, READ 1 SAMUEL 15:1-3. ✳ ✎

03 . Why did the Amalekites deserve such a severe punishment? Does the shocking nature of this text make it untrue?

AS A GROUP, READ 1 SAMUEL 15:7-15,20-23. ✳ ✎

04 . Yet again, Saul and his army only partially complied with the Lord's command. Why did they disobey this time? What was the Lord's reaction to this?

05 . Saul built a monument to himself. Based on this, what did he think about himself, and what did he think about God?

06 . Do you think Saul was truly surprised that his behaviors were sinful, or do you think he was attempting to make his disobedience seem more acceptable? Explain.

**NOW
LISTEN TO
THE WORDS**

(respond to God's Word)

apply the text

While we may not hear the words of God audibly from the prophet Samuel, we are reading Samuel's words in the Bible. Like Saul, we have heard directly from God and, in our modern context, can see His will through His Word. Before coming down too hard on Saul, let us consider times we have done the same things. Through social media, we might build monuments to ourselves. Through compromising with sin, we might be guilty of the same kind of disobedience. As we look to Saul, we can see our own reflections.

07 . Why is partial obedience to God insufficient? What is necessary instead?

08 . Inspired by the way Samuel guided Saul, what are some simple ways we as a group can encourage one another in the coming week?

09 . "To obey is better than sacrifice" (1 Sam. 15:22). In what areas are you substituting sacrifice for obedience?

CLOSE YOUR GROUP TIME IN PRAYER, REFLECTING ON WHAT YOU HAVE DISCUSSED. ✱╱

TO OBEY IS BETTER

01. _ _
02. _ _
03. _ _
04. _ _
05. _ _
06. _ _
07. _ _
08. _ _

01. _ _
02. _ _
03. _ _

04. _ _

saul
ISRAEL'S FIRST KING

known for

- Saul was physically impressive, standing a head taller than most Israelites **(1 Sam. 9:2)**.

- He was a valiant soldier, yet a paranoid and impulsive commander **(1 Sam. 13:3-4,10-12)**.

- He delivered the people of Jabesh-gilead from humiliation by the Ammonites **(1 Sam. 11:1-11)**.

- He reigned as Israel's king for forty-two years, yet in the end failed because he disobeyed God **(1 Sam. 15:17-29)**.

- Saul took David into his royal administration but later made several attempts to kill him in fits of jealous rage **(1 Sam. 18–21)**.

- Saul killed eighty-five priests and wiped out the priestly town of Nob suspecting the priests of conspiring with David **(1 Sam. 22:11-19)**.

- Saul visited the witch of En-dor in an effort to contact the dead prop Samuel for guidance **(1 Sam. 28)**.

- Battling the Philistines, Saul's three sons were killed and he was sever wounded. To avoid capture, Saul fell on his own sword **(1 Sam. 31)**.

basic facts

- Son of Kish, of the tribe of Benjamin, who became the first king of Israel.
- Name Saul means "asked for."
- Anointed as king by Samuel the prophet; publicly elected by a process of casting lots.
- Was 30 when he became king; ruled 42 years.

05 . Married to Ahinoam; ha children, including Jonat and Michal.

06 . Died in battle against Philistines; wounded by arrows, then fell on his sword.

PERSONAL STUDY 01.

(continue studying on your own)
Read 1 Samuel 13:6-14.

God expects us to reflect His holy character in our lives through obedience to His commands. King Saul chose to disobey God when he allowed his soldiers to take plunder from their battle with the Amalekites, and he also disobeyed when he spared the Amalekite king's life. Partial obedience is still disobedience.

01 . What excuses have you made for disobeying God in the past? Were you being honest with yourself at the time?

Obeying God is not always going to be the popular thing to do. It will not always be the culturally acceptable thing to do. It could cost you friends and even bring ridicule—but it could also make an eternal impact on your friends' lives. God expects us to obey Him. He gave us everything, even His life on the cross. What we lose in following Him is ultimately meaningless. What we gain lasts forever. Are you excelling in things that do not matter and failing in the one thing that matters forever?

Saul knew precisely what he ought to have done, and that is what makes his story so important. He knew God's instructions and still fell short. His disobedience had cascading effects that damaged him, his family, and even his entire nation. Our sin does not affect us alone. We are not a crowd of individuals. As the Church, we are God's people and our sin affects the body.

02 . How can disobedience on the part of believers cause others to discount the gospel or avoid listening to us?

03 . Are there ways that you could improve the example of faith you set for others through greater obedience to God?

The formation of Israel's monarchy led to renewed conflict between Israel and the Philistines. The Philistines continued to be militarily superior. Furthermore, their monopoly on iron also provided them with economic advantages. Israel was a predominately agricultural society, but its farmers were totally dependent on Philistine blacksmiths for making and repairing the tools they needed for farming.

Saul's victory over the Ammonites (1 Sam. 11:5-11) encouraged action against the Philistines. Saul had divided his army and placed his son Jonathan in command of one force. Jonathan, an aggressive commander, quickly attacked a nearby Philistine outpost. The Philistines assembled a massive military force to crush Israel once and for all. Panic seized the Israelite army. Many soldiers deserted. Anxious, Saul took over the role of priest and offered an unwarranted sacrifice—a sacrifice that did not follow God's commands and that displeased the Lord immensely. The prophet Samuel soundly denounced the king's rash action. The Philistine invaders sent three companies to attack the Israelites.

Displaying poor judgment, King Saul issued a rash vow that almost cost the life of his son. Nevertheless, the Philistine invasion was held back. Immediately thereafter, God instructed Saul to completely destroy the Amalekites. However, Saul failed to obey God fully. In this moment we can see how the actions of one person affect many others. As a result of Saul's disobedience to God, Saul and Samuel separated and never saw each other again. Even more significantly, God rejected Saul as king (1 Sam. 15:22-23). Saul's disobedience proved costly for him, his family, and the nation of Israel.

04 . In what ways have you been affected by the sins of someone else? As far as you know, how has your sin affected others?

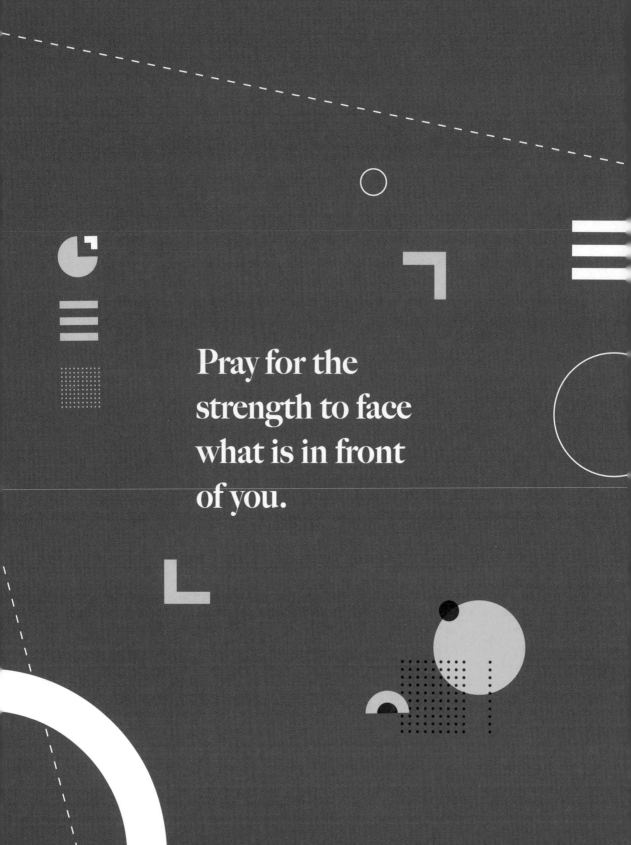

Pray for the
strength to face
what is in front
of you.

PERSONAL STUDY 02.

(continue studying on your own)
Read 1 Samuel 18:1-9; 19:11-17.

Prepare to watch jealousy utterly destroy someone in 1 Samuel 18 and 19. Jealousy not only shows a lack of gratitude, but also challenges the wisdom and provision of God.

In the beginning, David and Saul had a good working relationship. David was a skilled commander and fighter, as well as the best friend of Saul's son, Jonathan. Saul was initially pleased with David; David was not only loyal but also successful for the sake of Saul's kingdom. But soon Saul's attitude toward David soured.

Upon returning home from battle, the women offered their customary songs praising the men for their victories. Saul was praised for killing his thousands, and David was praised for killing his tens of thousands. Saul was jealous of David's praise and popularity, and it enraged him. Jealousy caused Saul to ignore the blessing that David was to his kingdom. Saul intently focused on his own diminished level of popularity with the people. Saul remembered what Samuel said in 1 Samuel 15:28, that someone better than him would be given his kingship, and realized it was about young David.

01 . Everyone experiences jealousy. As you think back through times when you have been jealous, what patterns do you see?

02 . What are some of the more helpful things you have told yourself in order to overcome the temptations associated with jealousy?

03 . Saul's jealousy impacted everyone around him. How does jealousy affect a Christian community?

Saul's jealousy drove him mad, and he attempted to kill David on many occasions. Saul sent men to kill David when he left his house the next morning (1 Sam. 19:11). But Michal, David's wife, was aware of her father's plan and, like her brother, warned David of the danger and urged him to flee before morning (1 Sam. 19:2). She helped David escape through a window, made a "dummy" to place in his bed as a decoy, and pretended he was sick (1 Sam. 19:12-14).

When his attempts to kill David failed, Saul had David followed and tried to use his daughter as a trap to keep David close. Saul's jealousy bubbled to the surface and eventually affected his kingdom and his family. Saul's family relationships and ability to govern came undone, all because he wanted what David had.

04 . List everything in your life that fills you with gratitude, and ask God to let that gratitude overwhelm your jealousy. Then, journal a prayer asking God to help you focus less on your jealousy and more on your calling.

You cannot know what others have faced, everything they currently face, or all they will face on the horizon. Especially on social media, people make their lives look amazing and, for obvious reasons, do not post their worst moments. The enemy would love to cause you to fixate on an illusion and neglect what God is calling you to do. Praise God for the awesome things He does through others and pray for the strength to face what is in front of you. You will not be evaluated one day based on how you would have done if you were given other people's challenges. So, let godly gratitude overwhelm your jealousy and step out boldly into what God has for you today.

PERSONAL STUDY ¦ 03.

(continue studying on your own)
Read 1 Samuel 31:1-13.

The final chapter of 1 Samuel resumes the account of the Philistine war
(1 Sam. 28–29). The Israelites were defeated and many were killed on Mount
Gilboa. Saul, wounded severely by archers in the battle, tried to convince his
terrified armor-bearer to run him through with a sword so that he could avoid
torture by the Philistines, but the armor-bearer could not do it. Saul felt he
had no choice other than to end his own life, and he fell on his own sword. His
corpse was publicly abused by the Philistines. Three of Saul's sons were also
killed in battle, which prepared the way for David to be king.

Saul's pride made him indifferent to the will of God and intensely jealous of
others. Eventually, it destroyed him. Despite the shameful end to Saul's legacy,
the people of Jabesh-gilead remembered how Saul had delivered them from the
Ammonites (11:1-11). They journeyed all night to Beth-shan, where Saul's body
and those of his sons had been impaled. At great risk to themselves, they stole
the bodies away and honorably buried them at Jabesh, where they mourned.
Saul had not honored the people or the Lord well, but the people honored him
as best they were able.

01 . If you were called to heaven tomorrow, what would your legacy be?
How would you be remembered?

02 . Why do we honor people at funerals even if they did not honor others?
Do someone's failures devalue their life?

Amidst the dark circumstances, a bright testimony of bravery shines through. Upon hearing of how the Philistines mistreated Saul's remains, some brave men journeyed all night to the wall of Beth-shan. Risking their lives, they gave a proper burial to Saul and his sons. Despite Saul's failures and disobedience, these men could not rest with the thought of their king and his sons being treated this way. Their bravery was recorded in Scripture as a testimony to their incredible respect for leadership even when that leadership failed. It was not just about Saul; it was about all that God would accomplish through the throne of Israel.

03 . How can you balance being responsible for your choices in life with the reality that you are not sovereign over your life?

Though this chapter ended with a bleak story, that story actually led the way to a beautiful hope. Do you remember the one whom God had chosen to take Saul's throne? David would not only follow and usher in a time of victory and peace, but would totally change what Saul's throne represented. The next king would be the ancestor to the true King. The next one to wear the crown was an ancestor to Jesus!

04 . What is it like to know that, despite epic failures like Saul's, God is still able to bring about something eternally good? What could God bring about from your failures?

Amidst the dark circumstances, a bright testimony of bravery shines through.

02

introduction

God often chooses the least qualified and most unlikely people to accomplish His will. This way, He clearly receives all of the glory for what He does through them. As the prophet Samuel was meeting the sons of Jesse, it was David, the young "runt," whom God told Samuel to anoint.

David was called by God's sovereign choice. The new king was chosen from a working-class family in a small town called Bethlehem. The new king was just a young man, a shepherd, and not someone who had worked his way up to the position. He was simply chosen by God. David had no clue that his life was about to change so dramatically. He was simply carrying out his responsibilities, faithfully serving his family.

David's kingship was unparalleled. Some have called him the greatest leader the world has ever known. While by no means perfect, by and large David's life can be summarized in one word: humility. For this reason and others, David is considered one of the great leaders and servants of Scripture.

How does pride lead to ruin? How does humility lead to honor?

Saul, the first king of Israel, was chosen by the people because of his impressive stature. Why did God choose David, someone who was such the opposite of Saul?

ISRAEL'S HUMBLE KING
david

The Spirit of the LORD spoke through me, his word was on my tongue. The God of Israel spoke; the Rock of Israel said to me, "The one who rules the people with justice, who rules in the fear of God, is like the morning light when the sun rises on a cloudless morning, the glisten of rain on sprouting grass."

2 SAMUEL 23:2-4

 **AFTER GOD'S OWN HEART**

GROUP DISCUSSION

(get started)

focus attention

List some qualities people look for in a person who is going to lead a nation. What is the most important quality in your mind?

 **ANOINTED KING**

explore the text

AS A GROUP, READ 1 SAMUEL 16:1-10. ✳ ✎

In 1 Samuel 15, Samuel told Saul that because of his disobedience, the kingdom would be taken from him and given to someone else. When he met the unlikely young shepherd whom God had chosen to replace Saul, even Samuel was surprised.

01 . Why did Samuel initially think Eliab was the Lord's choice? What's the twist here (see 1 Sam. 10:23-24)?

02 . What does verse 7 suggest about the qualities God counts as most important for His servants?

Eliab was outwardly impressive in the same way Saul was outwardly impressive (see 1 Sam. 10:23-24). However, God cares more about our hearts.

AS A GROUP, READ 1 SAMUEL 16:11-13. ✳ ✎

03 . What characteristic would seem to hinder David from being anointed as king (v. 11)?

God had been working behind the scenes in David's life in order to prepare him for his future role as king. Tending sheep helped prepare David to rule Israel. God intended for the king to care for people with the same compassion that a shepherd gives to the flock.

04 . What did David's faithfulness in watching the sheep say about his character? How did this prepare him for the future (see 1 Sam. 17:34-37; Ps. 23)?

apply the text

Throughout the Bible, God chooses unlikely people to join Him in His plans to redeem humanity from sin. You may not think of yourself as a likely candidate to lead others spiritually in any way, but the Bible is full of people with less than perfect backgrounds. It seems that these are the kinds of people God chooses—broken and imperfect, yet full of promise when they seek forgiveness, strive to do God's will, repent of past mistakes, and move on in the grace only God can provide.

05 . Who do you identify with most in this story: Samuel, Jesse, Jesse's sons, or David? Why?

06 . How might knowing that God has chosen you to serve Him change the way you view your place in this world?

CLOSE YOUR GROUP TIME IN PRAYER,
REFLECTING ON WHAT YOU HAVE DISCUSSED. *⁄

TENDING
THE SHEEP

01. _ _
02. _ _
03. _ _
04. _ _
05. _ _
06. _ _

01. _ _
02. _ _

david

ISRAEL'S HUMBLE KING

known for

- As a young man, David challenged and killed Goliath, a giant Philistine warrior, by trusting in the Lord to give him the victory **(1 Sam. 17).**
- David had to spend years as a bandit leader hiding from King Saul, who was determined to kill David **(1 Sam. 20–27).**
- After David became king of all Israel, he moved the ark of God to Jerusalem. God made a covenant with the king to establish David's kingdom forever **(2 Sam. 6–7).**
- David committed adultery with Bathsheba, then tried to cover up his sin by ensuring her husband (Uriah) was killed in battle **(2 Sam. 11).** He married Bathsheba and the couple had a son, Solomon, who later succeeded David as king **(2 Sam. 12:24; 1 Kings 1:32-35).**
- David wrote and collected many psalms; known as the "sweet psalmist of Israel" **(2 Sam. 23:1).**
- He is remembered as the ideal king and forerunner of the Messiah **(Isa. 9:6-7; Luke 1:30-33).**

basic facts

- Youngest son of Jesse of Bethlehem, who became Israel's second king and the most revered Israelite ruler in history.
- Name David means "beloved." Anointed at a young age by the prophet Samuel to become king in place of Saul; became king at age thirty.

03. Ruled as king forty years; seven years over Judah, thirty-three ye in Jerusalem over all Israel.

04. Married eight wives with whom he had eleven children (ten sons one daughter); had nine other sons by concubines.

05. Died at age seventy and buried in Jerusalem.

God sees all
YOUR
POTENTIAL

PERSONAL STUDY 01.

(continue studying on your own)
Read 1 Samuel 16:1-13.

God is sovereign, which means that He is the absolute authority in life—He has the right to make any decision that is consistent with His perfect character. God's choice of a new leader for Israel was David, which made David God's sovereign choice. As we will discover later, David would grow up, mature, and become a great king and leader. He would not be a perfect king and leader. Far from it. But he was still God's choice to lead.

01 . Who is one of the greatest leaders you've known or known about? Why is that person your choice?

David's arrival at his father's house was accompanied by the only physical description that is given of him. In one translation, David is described as being "ruddy." From the Hebrew, that means "dark, reddened complexion." The description also indicates he had good countenance. That is an internal description: "countenance" comes from the inside and is reflected on the outside. There are a lot of good-looking people who do not have good countenance.

Scripture also indicates he was handsome. Nevertheless, David was not God's choice because of his looks, but because of his love. However, we should not miss the fact that all of Jesse's sons were good-looking. Samuel was impressed with all of them, and would have been delighted to anoint any of them.

God's choice of David was based on his inner qualities. With the confirming words of God, "Anoint him, for he is the one" (v. 12), Samuel poured the oil on David's head, signifying that he was God's choice to be leader and king.

02 . What emotions or thoughts do you have knowing that God looks past your outward appearance and instead evaluates you based on your heart and character?

03 . List the names of people who have seen the untapped potential in you and helped you reach it.

This must have been the occasion David reflected on to write Psalm 23:5, "You anoint my head with oil; my cup overflows." In the same space that describes the anointing in 1 Samuel, it says, "The Spirit of the Lord came powerfully on David from that day forward" (16:13). This was mentioned because the position of king over Israel was, first and foremost, a spiritual position, which was not the case with the other neighboring kings. David needed spiritual resources to be king over God's people.

David's appointment wasn't instant. Many years passed between the time of David's anointing and the day he would officially become king. Instead, his anointing was a promise from God that one day David would lead Israel and be its king. David was God's choice.

Could God choose you to be a leader? Are you resisting His calling because you feel unworthy? Remember that God looks past who the world sees, and He sees the person we can become in relationship with Him. He knows our potential to be used by Him to do great things. God chose David. He may be choosing you too.

PERSONAL STUDY ┆ 02 .

(continue studying on your own)
Read 1 Samuel 18:1-4; 19:4-7; 20:8,12-13.

The first king of Israel was Saul. Crazed by jealousy, Saul tried repeatedly to kill David, but Saul's own children would sabotage him. David's best friend in the world was Jonathan, one of Saul's sons! Their friendship saved David's life and set the standard for authentic connection between friends.

01 . What percentage of the people who follow you on social media actually know you? What percentage of all social media posts do you believe are authentic, coming from the heart?

02 . What is the first step you could take to developing a deeper and more genuine friendship with someone in your social media network? What about someone in your church?

Genuine friendships are important (see Prov. 17:17; 18:24; 27:9). These kinds of connections are a vital part of being a Christian. Christians do not gather in a building to hear the same message at the same time for efficiency. Rather, we are the people of God who are filled with the Spirit of God and our interconnected gifts are important to how we fulfill the mission of God. We live out God's will alongside one another and protect each other like David and Jonathan.

This friendship between David and Jonathan has been taken out of context by some people in our culture to spin some radically unbiblical myths, but basic reading comprehension of the Bible will prepare you to dispel those if they arise.

03 . How have you been a friend to someone recently? What benefit did you receive by being a friend?

The web of relationships around Saul and David was remarkably complex. Saul's insecurities led him to sometimes "need" David, yet other times despise and envy him. At one point, Saul offered his daughter Merab to David as his wife if David would continue to fight Saul's enemies. Saul hoped David would be killed in battle. David insisted he did not deserve the king's daughter, but another of Saul's daughters named Michal fell in love with David, so Saul offered her hand in marriage in exchange for the deaths of one hundred Philistines. David killed two hundred of the enemy and married Michal, a move that only further incensed Saul.

David's friendship with Jonathan further complicated matters. Jonathan knew that Saul intended to kill David, so he spoke up in David's defense and intervened to protect David from Saul. In all of this, David was challenged to respect the authority and office of the kingship, maintain loyalty to a dear friend, and love his wife. Talk about drama!

04 . Have you ever found yourself in a similarly complicated web of relationships? If you could go back in time to those conflicts, what would you do differently?

05 . Practically speaking, what is the difference between honoring other people and pleasing other people? Which did David do, and why?

PERSONAL STUDY 03.

(continue studying on your own)
Read 1 Samuel 24:1-7a,11-12,16-22.

As a Christian, you will often see big differences between your values and the world's values. For example, retaliation seems to be a widely accepted practice when we feel like justice cannot be served any other way, but Christians are committed to letting the Lord be the one to bring justice. In this story, David had an opportunity to take revenge against Saul for attempting to kill him, but he instead chose to follow the Lord's commands.

01 . What is the hardest part about not taking action against someone who has harmed you?

Instead of killing Saul when he was defenseless, David cut off a piece of Saul's robe to show that he could have done worse, but didn't. David's men saw Saul's arrival in the cave as the fulfillment of some sort of prophecy. David, they thought, should take advantage of this opportunity to kill Saul.

02 . When have you been tempted to take action against someone, only to back off and show that person mercy instead? What feelings did you have after you made that decision?

Although David acted with mercy toward Saul, he soon regretted even cutting his robe and told his followers he would never hurt God's anointed king. When David announced to Saul that he had spared his life, Saul declared David more righteous than himself. David took an oath not to attack Saul's family. David's speech persuaded his men, and none of them tried to kill Saul either.

David's decision is puzzling for many. We live in a world in which revenge and retaliation are not only exercised, but expected. Clearly, David's decision was motivated by something higher than the morals of the day. It can only be explained by faith that God had put Saul in his position and, therefore, should be respected.

03 . How do we show respect to people we disagree with, yet who hold leadership roles in our school, church, or country?

David knew that vengeance was the Lord's. He did not need to take the situation into his own hands. He trusted God to bring justice and peace. Likewise, we can trust that God will right every wrong done to us. As Christians, we must forgive our enemies and pray for them. By trying to take our own revenge, we declare that we do not trust in a sovereign, all-powerful God to judge and punish wrongdoers. We have no need to take action against those who persecute us; instead, we can leave that in God's hands, trusting that He is the righteous Judge who knows our hearts, sees our actions, and brings wrongdoers to justice. David knew this well and lived by his belief in a God who makes all things right. We can do the same.

04 . To whom could you show mercy, even though this person may be wrong in his or her actions or words toward you?

But I tell you, love
your enemies and
pray for those who
persecute you.

MATTHEW 5:44

AND PRAY

03

introduction

Life can be an onslaught of difficult choices and it is normal to feel over-whelmed from time to time. The beautiful news is that we are not left on our own. God gives us wisdom from His Word. With godly wisdom, a series of difficult choices can become a parade of godly triumphs. When God asked Solomon what gift he would like, Solomon responded with a request for great wisdom to lead God's people. God granted the request—and more.

Solomon showed himself to be a phenomenally wise king who, for much of his reign, was concerned with staying humble, ruling his people according to God's ways, and maintaining a strong per-sonal relationship with God. Solomon was David's son, and as we study his life, we see how Solomon was the fulfillment of promises God made to David.

Solomon was far from perfect and would lose his way for a long season. However, in his wisdom and leadership, he foreshadowed the perfect King to come.

Who is the wisest person you know?

To whom do you turn when you need someone to help you make an important decision?

ISRAEL'S WISE KING
solomon

Lord my God, you have now made your servant king in my father David's place. Yet I am just a youth with no experience in leadership... So give your servant a receptive heart to judge your people and to discern between good and evil. For who is able to judge this great people of yours?

1 KINGS 3:7,9

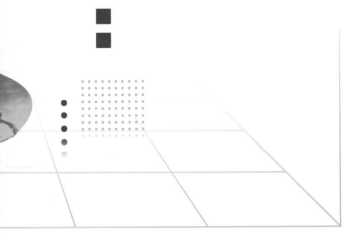

WISE AND UNDERSTANDING HEART

GROUP DISCUSSION

〈get started〉

focus attention

What is the number one source people turn to for wisdom today? What happens when our source of wisdom is flawed?

ADMINISTER JUSTICE

explore the text

AS A GROUP, READ 1 KINGS 3:1-9. ✻ ╱

01 . How would you respond if God offered to give you anything you asked? Why?

02 . Why did Solomon desire wisdom above anything else? What does this reveal about him and his relationship with God?

03 . What situation in your life right now makes you feel inadequate? What difference has God's wisdom made in how you have (or have not) dealt with that situation?

AS A GROUP, READ 1 KINGS 3:10-15. ✻ ╱

04 . What does God's willingness to give Solomon more than he asked for reveal about His nature? How have you witnessed God's generosity in your own life?

God was pleased that Solomon's request centered on the successful accomplishment of God's calling rather than on worldly or self-centered desires. God listed three requests a self-focused king might have made in Solomon's situation: long life, riches, or the death of enemies. God promised to give Solomon a wise and understanding heart. He granted Solomon's request above and beyond what was asked, beginning with the kind of "heart" that would equip Solomon to rule effectively. Because Solomon asked for things on behalf of God's people (see 3:9), God gave the honor and prestige of a worthy monarch.

apply the text

Even though Solomon did not ask for riches, God gave him riches along with wisdom. God does not promise to give you wealth, but He does promise to meet all your needs. God wants you to put Him first in your life, to fill your mind with His desires, to imitate Him, and to serve and obey Him in everything. Then He will give you what you need from day to day.

05 . In what ways do you value living with godly wisdom more than pursuing wealth or achievements?

06 . What are some blessings that might accompany God-given wisdom, and how might you use those blessings in God's service?

CLOSE YOUR GROUP TIME IN PRAYER, REFLECTING ON WHAT YOU HAVE DISCUSSED. ✱✎

MY
FATHER
DAVID

01. _ _
02. _ _
03. _ _
04. _ _
05. _ _
06. _ _
07. _ _

01. _ _
02. _ _
03. _ _

solomon
ISRAEL'S WISE KING

known for

- His renown for wisdom included difficult judicial decisions **(1 Kings 3:16-28)**, literary works (three thousand proverbs and over one thousand songs/psalms; 1 Kings 4:32), and administrative skills **(1 Kings 4:1-28)**.

- Solomon completed great construction projects—the palace and the temple of the Lord **(1 Kings 5–7)**, using slave labor **(1 Kings 9:15-23)**.

- Solomon had a troubling relationship with the queen of Sheba **(1 Kings 10:1-13)**.

- He extended Israel's dominance over surrounding kingdoms further than any Israelite ruler before or after him **(1 Kings 4:20-21)**.

- In his years straying from God's will, Solomon took seven hundred wives and housed even more women in an ungodly way **(1 Kings 7:8)**.

- Solomon's foreign wives persuaded him to establish idol worship in Israel, angering God **(1 Kings 11:1-10)**.

- In his later years, Solomon developed serious questions about life's ultimate meaning in the Book of Ecclesiastes.

basic facts

- Son of David and Bathsheba who succeeded his father as king and greatly extended Israel's influence in the ancient world.
- Name Solomon relates to the Hebrew word for "peace."
- Also known as Jedidiah, meaning "beloved of Yahweh," a name given him by Nathan the prophet.

04. Reigned as king of Israel for forty years.
05. His age at death not indicated in Scripture but estimated to be around age sixty.

PERSONAL STUDY 01.

(continue studying on your own)
Read 1 Kings 3:16-28.

Solomon's new-found wisdom would soon be tested by two prostitutes. This story is one of the best known in the whole Bible. Israel's kings were sometimes called upon to settle particularly difficult cases (see 2 Sam 12:1-6; 14:1-11), and this situation is quite perplexing.

Two prostitutes had given birth to babies. One woman smothered her child in the night, then switched babies while the other woman slept. Now both women claimed the living child as their own. Without witnesses or evidence, Solomon had to devise some way to solve the case, exercise wisdom, and provide justice.

01 . When have you been called on to make a difficult decision? How did you decide on a course of action?

Kings were the highest recourse for justice, expected to be in a place of public access to take up the case of the widow, the orphan, and the oppressed. Solomon quickly produced his own evidence. He decided to try the case based on the women's maternal instincts and human compassion. Calling for a sword, he ordered the child cut in two, with each woman getting an equal share. The real mother, who already cared enough for her child to plead her case before the king, acted out of "compassion for her son." She begged Solomon to give the baby to the other woman so that the child could live. In startling contrast, the dishonest woman was willing to take her "half." Her cruelty was revealed, just as the other mother's kindness emerged.

02 . List some past incidents in which you have been lied to. Based on this text, how might Solomon have responded in each incident?

The relationship between the two women was obviously not good, which should not be surprising considering the circumstances in which they lived. Solomon's judgment did not deal with the circumstances of the death of the child or with the various accusations being made. His concern was with the bonding relationship of a mother and her child. The living child had no father, but the true mother was determined to care for her child.

Once Solomon knew the identity of the true mother, he did not engage in further punishments. Rather, the compassionate woman was simply given the child. He had the insight to see the difference between just and unjust persons even when he had no witnesses or evidence.

When this verdict became public knowledge, the nation revered their king (see v. 28). This respect came from the knowledge that wisdom like Solomon's could come only from God. Israel now understood that "God's wisdom was in him to carry out justice." If so, the nation would flourish under his leadership.

03 . What decision or situation are you facing in which you could use the kind of wisdom Solomon demonstrated?

Lord God of Israel, there is no God like you in heaven above or on earth below, who keeps the gracious covenant with your servants who walk before you with all their heart.

1 KINGS 8:23

PERSONAL
STUDY ⌐ 02.

(continue studying on your own)
Read 1 Kings 8:22-43.

Solomon started the foundation of the temple in Jerusalem during the fourth year of his reign. The structure required seven years, intense manpower, and a great deal of money to finish.

Eleven months after its completion, during the Festival of Booths, Solomon assembled Israel's leadership in Jerusalem where he held a national ceremony to dedicate the temple and rededicate the nation to God. He had the ark of the Lord's covenant brought into the temple. The priests placed the ark in the inner sanctuary, the most holy place. God's glory filled the building in the form of a cloud, showing God's presence and showing His approval of the temple.

Solomon thanked God for how He had saved his people in the past (see vv. 12-21). Then, he asked God to save Israel in the future (see vv. 22-43).

01 . According to 1 Kings 8:23, what is it about God that motivates Him to love and keep a people for Himself?

02 . Is it possible to have an opinion of God that is too high? Based on what you pray for and the way you pray, have you been underestimating God?

One might conclude that a God worthy of such a temple operated out of obligation or guilt. Solomon's prayer reveals that the one true God relates to His people in an entirely different kind of way. Not obligation, not legalism, nor a desire to control others for personal gain motivates God. Every miracle, saving act, or law flows from divine mercy and grace. It is for this reason that Solomon understood that God stands ready to hear people's prayers, to forgive their sins, and to initiate or restore their relationship with Him. He hears those who pour out their needs and problems to Him.

03 . In your current walk with the Lord, are you motivated to pray? Why or why not? What characteristics of God highlighted in Solomon's prayer stand out to you in this moment?

Solomon's prayer reveals a few things about God that should influence the way you pray and the things you pray for. According to Solomon's prayer:

•   God is faithful to keep His promises.

•   God listens to our prayers.

•   God responds to our prayers by forgiving us and acting to help us.

How different prayer would be if God were not faithful, a good listener, responsive, or forgiving! May these attributes of God inspire and motivate you to pray to a loving and faithful God who longs for a relationship with you!

PERSONAL STUDY : 03.

(continue studying on your own)
Read 1 Kings 11:1-13.

When it comes to resolving conflict, compromise by all parties is often required. Finding common ground heals broken relationships. It can restore relations between fighting nations. It can reduce disagreements between husbands and wives. Reaching a win-win solution can make friendships stronger. Spiritual compromise, however, is always wrong. When we ignore God's clear statements of right and wrong, we sin. God holds Christians accountable for their sins regardless of position, age, or previous faithfulness.

When he was dealing with people outside of his family, Solomon was incredibly successful. People recognized him as a man of great wisdom. The king completed extensive building projects and accumulated great wealth. He expanded David's kingdom and established peaceful relations with the surrounding nations.

Despite these outward achievements, however, Solomon failed in his personal life. Moral and spiritual weaknesses increasingly characterized the end of his life and rule. He failed to honor God and keep love for Him above his own desires. Solomon's failures had disastrous results for his family and the nation. God held Solomon accountable for his sins and judged him for his disobedience. His negative example encourages us to guard against any spiritual compromise.

01. Compare Solomon's actions with Deuteronomy 7:1-4; 17:17. What specific commands did Solomon disobey?

Solomon's spiritual downfall started with a departure from God's laws. He abandoned wholehearted love for God and obedience to Him. One compromise led to another.

02 . What role did Solomon's wives play in his idolatry? What can you learn from Solomon's example about the way others can influence your spiritual life?

03 . Tolerating idolatry in his own household eventually led to Solomon's own participation in idolatry. What does this teach us about sin?

Solomon's tragic end is puzzling. This king had everything going for him, but he seemed to waste it by giving in to his own desires. The Lord blessed him with more than he asked. He had a glorious kingdom, riches, wisdom, and fame. Yet Solomon allowed sin to remain all around him, and it eventually corrupted him. He started with a good foundation, but he did not remain faithful to God. His small compromises led to great sins. His impressive accomplishments were overshadowed by his unimpressive character.

04 . In what part of your life do you know you are consciously and willfully disobeying a direct command from God?

05 . What steps do you need to take to remain faithful to God and avoid spiritual compromise?

I will tear the kingdom away from you and give it all to your servant.

1 Kings 11:11

04

introduction

Does your family determine your destiny?

Thankfully, the answer to that question is "No." Asa's father and grandfather were sinful men who led Judah away from the Lord. His grandmother Maacah, the queen mother of Judah, set up an obscene image of the Canaanite goddess Asherah. From this lineage, you might expect King Asa to be a horrible person. Yet we are told in 2 Chronicles 14:2, "Asa did good and right in the sight of the Lord his God."

Asa reigned for forty-one years as one of Judah's most godly kings. He was a reformer, leading the Southern Kingdom back to the worship of the one true God. His leadership was so effective that many from the northern ten tribes of Israel immigrated to his kingdom and joined in the revival of his days. At the end, however, Asa stumbled, and the last five years of his reign were out of step with the godliness that had characterized it up to that point. The civil war with Israel resurfaced, and instead of trusting God, Asa trusted in an alliance with the pagan king of Aram.

What are some qualities or habits you have inherited from your parents or grandparents?

How is your life similar to, or different from, the lives lived by your parents and grandparents?

JUDAH'S IDOL - DESTROYING KING
asa

Then Asa cried out to the Lord his God: "Lord, there is no one besides you to help the mighty and those without strength. Help us, Lord our God, for we depend on you, and in your name we have come against this large army. Lord, you are our God. Do not let a mere mortal hinder you."

2 CHRONICLES 14:11

CHOP DOWN THE IDOL

GROUP DISCUSSION

(get started)

focus attention

Have you ever felt the need to make a clean break with your past? Explain.

CRUSH AND BURN THE OBSCENE

explore the text

AS A GROUP, READ 2 CHRONICLES 14:1-5. ✳ ✎

01 . What is Asa's overall legacy? How did Asa's faithfulness impact the everyday lives of the people?

02 . Note the phrase "seek the Lord" in verse 4. What does it look like, in basic terms, for people to seek the Lord? What happens to societies that seek the Lord? What is the effect on both?

03 . What forms of idol worship are prevalent in our culture today? What is appealing about them?

04 . Why do you think we so easily fall into the trap of giving our hearts to idols? What are some of the excuses we use for worshiping idols?

For those in Asa's day, the phrase "seek the Lord" described how one was to respond to God. It involved more than a specific act of seeking God's help and guidance—it stood for one's whole duty toward God. In other words, it meant knowing God and being wholeheartedly devoted to Him. In Asa's time, this meant repentance from idol worship and the destruction of all that might have been a representation of that worship.

apply the text

The "good and right" that Asa did was to remove the foreign (Canaanite) altars, high places, sacred pillars, and the Asherim. Not only did he remove the negative influences of Baal worship, but Asa also commanded Judah to seek the Lord and study His Word (the Law). As a result of Asa's "clean-up" campaign, the land was undisturbed for ten years, and, instead of putting their energies into war, they were able to build the nation's infrastructure. God had redefined Asa's family legacy.

05 . Have you allowed your family background to keep you from serving the Lord? How might you make a break with the past and serve the Lord today?

06 . Idolatry is the worship of something created rather than the Creator. What man-made things come between you and God?

07 . What would our life look like if we truly chose to worship God above everything else? How would this look different than how you live life now?

CLOSE YOUR GROUP TIME IN PRAYER, REFLECTING ON WHAT YOU HAVE DISCUSSED. ✳╱

THE KINGDOM EXPERIENCED PEACE

01. _ _
02. _ _
03. _ _
04. _ _
01. _ _
02. _ _
03. _ _

asa

JUDAH'S IDOL-DESTROYING KING

known for

Asa led Judah in a national movement of repentance and renewal. The movement included the removal of pagan altars, idols, and shrines, as well as the rebuilding of fortifications around key cities to protect against foreign invaders **(2 Chron. 14:2-7; 15:1-19)**.

Threatened by an invasion from the south of a million-man army of Cushites, King Asa sought the Lord's help and repelled the invaders with his much smaller army of 300,000 warriors **(2 Chron. 14:8-15)**.

In the thirty-sixth year of Asa's reign, the king of the Northern Kingdom declared war on Judah. Instead of seeking the Lord's help, Asa made an alliance with the king of Aram (Syria) to attack his rival from the north. While Asa succeeded in forcing the Northern Kingdom to withdraw, the king received a prophetic rebuke for not trusting in the Lord **(2 Chron. 16:1-10)**.

Asa's lack of trust in the Lord continued when he developed a severe foot disease. Whether the disease cut short the king's life is unclear, but he sought help only from physicians and not from God **(2 Chron. 16:12-13)**.

basic facts

- Great-grandson of Solomon, who succeeded his father Abijam as ruler of the Southern Kingdom of Judah in 911 BC.
- Name Asa means "physician" or "healing."
- Reigned forty-one years as king.

04 . Married to Azubah, who gave birth to Asa's son and successor, Jehoshaphat.

05 . Developed severe foot disease two years before his death.

06 . Buried in a tomb he made for himself in Jerusalem.

PERSONAL STUDY 01.

(continue studying on your own)
Read 2 Chronicles 14:8-15.

In 2 Chronicles 13, the army of Judah was surrounded, but God helped them to defeat rebellious Israel. And, in this one battle, half a million soldiers of Israel were slain. Building on this victory, Abijah (Asa's father) fortified his troops and "grew strong" (13:21). Though Abijah's reign was short, he left behind a well-organized and experienced army that trusted the Lord and saw victory. It is worth noting that in their battle with Israel, the soldiers of Judah "cried out to the Lord" (13:14), though there is no record of Abijah himself crying to the Lord.

The 300,000 soldiers of Judah, Asa's inherited army, were equipped for battle and skilled at hand-to-hand combat. The 280,000 soldiers of Benjamin were skilled with bows and arrows, which allowed them to attack from a distance. All 580,000 were "valiant warriors" according to verse 8.

01 . Though Asa's army was mighty, it was vastly outnumbered against Zerah's one million men and three hundred chariots. Despite the odds against him, what advantage did Asa have?

Before going into battle, Asa "cried out to the Lord his God" (v. 11). The words "we depend on you" show a humble heart that is ready to give full credit for the coming victory to God. The words, "in your name we have come against this large army" show Asa's full motivation. His proclamation "you are our God" professed total loyalty to the Lord and all of these statements combined give the clear case for why God gave them victory.

02 . Which words from Asa's prayer in verse 11 most inspire you? Which phrase will you use in your own prayer life in the coming week?

Asa called upon the Lord as the one who could help the powerless against the mighty. Interestingly, the literal Hebrew reads, "It is not with you to help between the great and him that has no strength." The meaning is that the strong as well as the weak need the Lord's assistance to gain victory. In this situation the appeal is to the Lord to help the weak.

As a result of their trust in God, Asa and the armies of Judah saw a total victory. According to the text, God caused the Cushite army to flee. Asa and the troops were able to follow and defeat them, bringing back plunder from the nearby cities around Gerar.

03 . Comparing your prayers to Asa's, what has been missing from your prayer life? Having you been tapping into your own strength instead of God's?

PERSONAL STUDY 02.

(continue studying on your own)
Read 2 Chronicles 15:1-19.

As Asa celebrated an incredible victory against a far greater opponent, he gave glory to God. The Spirit prompted the prophet Azariah to tell Asa, "The Lord is with you when you are with him (v.2)." This message holds true even today.

01. How can victories lead you to forget about God? Why is it important for you to worship not only when you need God desperately, but when you are blessed by God abundantly?

Asa immediately did two things in response to Azariah's prophecy. First, he removed "the abhorrent idols from the whole land of Judah and Benjamin and from the cities he had captured in the hill country of Ephraim" (v. 8). The little phrase, "took courage" suggests that this was something he had already been thinking about, but was afraid to do. Secondly, Asa restored (renovated) the altar of the Lord. Both are significant.

When we set out to tear down the idols in our lives, we need to be careful that we do not simply replace them with new idols. If our focus is on anything but God Himself—even on serving Him—we are idolatrous. God wants us to turn away from sin and turn toward Him, the only true Victor over sin.

02. Is there anything taking first place in your life besides God? How might a trusted friend answer that question about you?

They had
sought him with
all their heart,
and he was
found by them.
So the Lord
gave them rest
on every side.

2 Chronicles 15:15

Asa gathered together all of Judah and Benjamin (the two tribes that made up the Southern Kingdom known as Judah), as well as people from three of the tribes of the Northern Kingdom (Israel). The explanation given here is significant: "They had defected to him from Israel in great numbers when they saw that the Lord his God was with him" (v. 9). Asa sealed this new era of following God with a special sacrifice of seven hundred oxen and seven thousand sheep from the spoils of the battle. Together, they made a covenant with God to seek Him with all their hearts and souls. Asa's example was followed by the people, and a great revival and time of peace resulted.

In his pursuit of holy obedience, Asa also removed Maacah from the position of queen mother because of the terrible idol she built and worshiped. Asa's actions showed his wholehearted devotion to the Lord as the main authority in his life, especially since honoring family elders was almost demanded in his culture. Not only did he demote the queen mother, but he personally cut down her horrible idol, broke it into pieces, and then burned it. However, verse 17 tells us that the high places were not removed from Israel, indicating that as wonderful as this revival was, it didn't reunify the nation or deal with the sinful worship of Israel (the northern ten tribes who were under a different king). Even so, in Asa we see a breath of fresh air as the wind of the Spirit blew through Judah and rekindled the flame of faith.

03 . Have you, like Asa, utterly destroyed the idols in your life, or have you left some behind? What idols might you need to remove?

PERSONAL STUDY 03.

(continue studying on your own)
Read 2 Chronicles 16:1-14.

Asa was a godly king, and for the early part of his reign, he led the people as no one had since David. Unfortunately, he did not finish as he started. In the thirty-sixth year of Asa's reign, his devotion and trust was again tested, and this time he slipped spiritually.

> 01 . What heroes from your past failed before your eyes? Were you holding them to an unrealistic standard that you could never match?

Baasha, the wicked king of the northern ten tribes of Israel, took over Ramah, a city that served as a gateway between the two kingdoms. Most likely, Baasha tried to stem the tide of defections from Israel to Judah that Asa's good and godly reign had produced. Since the high road to and from Jerusalem passed through Ramah, he made this border town a military station in order to keep anyone from leaving or coming to King Asa.

Asa, instead of seeking the Lord or trusting Him to deliver, made a hasty, ill-advised treaty with the pagan king of Aram, Ben-hadad, using the temple treasures as payment. Ben-hadad accepted the payoff and attacked Israel, forcing Baasha to leave Ramah to defend his territories. In the short run, Asa's plan appeared successful.

> 02 . Asa tried to do God's work for Him in verses 1-6. In what ways have you stepped out of line with what you knew God expected of you in the past? Pray for patience to wait upon the Lord in the future.

Hanani's message was a simple one: "Because you depended on the king of Aram and have not depended on the Lord your God, the army of the king of Aram has escaped from you." He reminded Asa of the victory God gave early in his reign, because "you depended on the Lord." The implication was that if Asa had trusted the Lord, God would have delivered both Baasha and Ben-hadad into his hands and two of his enemies would be gone. Now, instead of removing Ben-hadad as an enemy, Asa had strengthened him with the wealth of Judah—a mistake that would come back to haunt him. Hanani closed his rebuke with a powerful reminder of God's heart toward His people: "The eyes of the Lord roam throughout the earth to show himself strong for those who are wholeheartedly devoted to him." What a powerful promise this is! And yet, for Asa it was a haunting reminder of why he had missed a blessing.

Instead of receiving this rebuke from God with a humble, repentant heart, Asa became angry and threw this messenger of the Lord into prison. God alone knows what the outcome would have been if Asa had repented in humility and asked the Lord's forgiveness. Instead, he bowed his back and refused to be instructed.

Sin always has consequences. However, it seems that the greatest consequences in our lives are not for acts of sin, but for the failure to repent when we are directly confronted by the Lord with our sin. That was certainly the case with Asa.

When God confronts us with sin, His intent is that we quickly repent and turn back to Him. The wonderful news, thanks to the gospel of Jesus Christ, is that He is ready to welcome us back when we do.

03 . Verse 10 tells us that "Asa mistreated some of the people at that time." Describe the correlation between sins in your life and the ways in which you have mistreated others.

05

introduction

In times of trouble, is prayer your first response, or your last resort? Trouble is unavoidable, and we usually don't take prayer seriously enough. Consider just how amazing the concept of prayer is: created people calling out to our Creator and watching Him use our prayers in His perfect plan. Why do we not pray sooner when trouble strikes? A wonderful portion of Scripture that drives this point home is 2 Kings 18–19, which concerns a man named Hezekiah. His story reveals that prayer does what nothing else can.

Hezekiah began his reign as king of Judah during the third year of King Hoshea, the last king of Israel. In the fourteenth year of Hezekiah's reign, the Assyrian King Sennacherib began his military campaign into the Southern Kingdom (Judah). This included a siege against Jerusalem. Unlike the kings of the Northern Kingdom, however, Hezekiah trusted in the Lord God. Not one of the kings of Judah—either before or after his time—was like him. He did what was right in the Lord's sight just as his ancestor David did. Hezekiah knew his hope for the future rested ultimately on the Lord and His saving power. This king relied on the Lord for help.

We do we tend to rely on human strength before trusting in God? Is it just forgetfulness, or is it something spiritually darker?

JUDAH'S PRAYING KING
hezekiah

Then Hezekiah turned his face to the wall and prayed to the Lord, "Please, Lord, remember how I have walked before you faithfully and wholeheartedly and have done what pleases you."

2 KINGS 20:2-3

 **RELY ON THE LORD**

GROUP DISCUSSION

(get started)
focus attention

What causes Christians to give up hope?
Why do we sometimes focus more on
discouragement than on the truth?

ENTHRONED
BETWEEN THE
CHERUBIM

explore the text

AS A GROUP, READ 2 KINGS 18:28-32. ✳ ✎

01 . Suppose you were a Hebrew standing on the wall. How would you feel after hearing Rabshakeh's words?

02 . Have you encountered a "Rabshakeh," someone who has tried to discourage you and tempt you to give up your trust in the Lord, claiming it was in order to rescue you? How did you respond?

AS A GROUP, READ 2 KINGS 19:1-7. ✳ ✎

03 . What was Hezekiah's first response when he heard what Rabshakeh had said (vv. 1-2)? What did this response say about his character and relationship with the Lord?

To tear one's clothes and put on itchy sackcloth was an outward sign of intense grief. According to verse 37 of the previous chapter, the court secretary, the court historian, and the man in charge of the palace had all torn their clothes as well. Hezekiah's hope in verse 4 was that the Lord would hear what had been said about Him and rebuke the one who said it.

AS A GROUP, READ 2 KINGS 19:14-19. ✳ ✎

04 . What did Hezekiah do with the threatening letter from Sennacherib? Why did he do this?

05 . What reason did Hezekiah give for God to save His people? How should this impact your own prayers?

apply the text

The psalmist says, "The Lord has heard my plea for help; the Lord accepts my prayer" (Ps. 6:9). The Lord can accomplish infinitely more than we would ever dare to ask or hope. His mighty power is at work within us. What an incredible thought! The God who created the universe loves us. He cares for us. He fights our battles while we keep silent. Nothing is impossible for Him. Whatever seemingly hopeless situation we find ourselves in, God can rescue us. May He be who we turn to first in such moments, not last.

06 . What is one situation in your life that has seemed so hopeless that you have stopped praying about it?

07 . What are some specific ways the story of Hezekiah should influence your prayer life?

08 . How can our group support you in prayer this week?

CLOSE YOUR GROUP TIME IN PRAYER,
REFLECTING ON WHAT YOU HAVE DISCUSSED. ✶✓

THE SURVIVING REMNANT

01. _ _
02. _ _
03. _ _
04. _ _
05. _ _

01. _ _
02. _ _
03. _ _
04. _ _

hezekiah
JUDAH'S PRAYING KING

known for

- Put spiritual reforms into place in Judah. He removed idolatrous shrines. He renewed temple worship and Passover celebration **(2 Chron. 29–31)**.

- In 701 BC, Hezekiah refused to pay tribute to the Assyrian Empire and faced an attack on the city of Jerusalem. Isaiah counseled the king to trust in the Lord's protection, which the Lord delivered by miraculously striking down 185,000 Assyrian warriors **(2 Kings 18–19)**.

- Hezekiah commissioned the digging of a 1,750-foot tunnel in the bedrock underneath Jerusalem. **(2 Chron. 32:2-4;30)**.

- When Hezekiah was deathly ill, Isaiah told him to put his house in order. After he repented, the Lord gave him 15 more years **(2 Kings 20:1-11)**.

- Hezekiah showed off all of his "treasure house" to envoys from Babylon. Isaiah prophesied that Hezekiah's foolish action would lead to Babylon taking Jerusalem and the Israelites into captivity **(1 Kings 20:12-19)**.

basic facts

- Son and successor of Judah's King Ahaz; his mother's name was Abi (or Abijah).
- Name Hezekiah means "Yahweh (the Lord) is my strength."
- Became king at age twenty five; ruled in Jerusalem for twenty-nine years.
- Lived during the time of Isaiah's prophetic ministry and the height of the Assyrian Empire.

05 . Became critically ill at age thirty-nine; told by Isaiah to prepare to die, but prayed for deliverance and lived fifteen extra years.

06 . Died at age fifty-four; buried alongside his ancestors in Jerusalem.

PERSONAL STUDY 01.

(continue studying on your own)
Read 2 Kings 18:1-8.

Judah was in bad shape when Hezekiah, the "Strength of Jehovah," ascended to the throne at the age of twenty-five after the death of his father in 728 BC. The political situation was humiliating. God's people continued to make payments to the pagan nation of Assyria as their former king Ahaz had established. Shockingly, God's people actually wanted this to continue because they believed it served to protect Israel and gave them a bond of union with Assyria's "Great King," which in essence made the Israelites slaves.

The priests were largely corrupt, and most of the prophets abused their office for selfish and dishonorable ends. Because these false teachers did not care how their teachings affected people and only wanted money, their false prophecies led people astray. The true prophets, faithful to their duty, were public enemies, while their rivals were held up as patriots.

01 . When have you recently witnessed or experienced injustice? Do you see it growing more or less prevalent today? Explain.

The public turned against the faithful, and the servants of God had to hide to protect their own lives. The majority of the people were poor, the rich were selfish and oppressive, and the judges were corrupt. All of society was poisoned by superstitious beliefs. The government was torn in two. One party urged a treaty with Egypt; another urged that the payments to Assyria continue; and a third stood up for national independence. Hezekiah had no light task before him to guide public affairs, and he was only twenty-five!

"Hezekiah relied on the Lᴏʀᴅ God of Israel,"...

2 KINGS 18:5

THE GOD OF ISRAEL

02 . What made the task of uniting the people much more difficult for a king like Hezekiah? What kinds of skills would he need in order to be successful?

As king, Hezekiah was inclined to seek peaceful means of resolution rather than violence. Though he could wrestle cities from the Philistines and defend Jerusalem in war, he gave his heart to the working for the internal welfare of his kingdom. Fond of farming pursuits, like his grandfather Uzziah, Hezekiah had great herds and flocks and built shepherds' towers for their protection.

Vineyards, olive yards, and cornfields were Hezekiah's delight. His tender religious sensibility and poetic genius—not seen since King David—are found in the hymn he composed after his recovery from a deadly sickness. His love of culture displayed itself in his passion for the preservation of the religious writings of his nation. Descended from Zechariah, Hezekiah inherited a high enthusiasm for the ancient faith. In direct contrast to his father, who had favored everything Assyrian, Hezekiah gave himself passionately to whatever was best for the people he led, and devoted his life to the restoration of the worship of Jehovah and the purification of the land from the false beliefs which Ahaz had introduced.

03 . How might Hezekiah's love for his nation, and a passion to see God worshiped and pagan influences removed, set the stage for the people to return to God in their hearts and lives?

04 . Have you turned from God in any area of your life? In what way do you, like the people of Hezekiah's day, need to repent of any wrongdoing and seek God wholeheartedly?

PERSONAL STUDY 02.

(continue studying on your own)
Read 2 Chronicles 29:1-36.

The Law was King Hezekiah's guiding star in public as well as private. The prophets were his honored and cherished counselors. Intelligent, refined, humble, and godly, Hezekiah took measures to collect and arrange the sacred books. He appointed a royal commission to gather the materials that now form the Book of Proverbs. Jewish tradition also gives him credit for collecting of the prophecies of Isaiah and the preserving the Book of Ecclesiastes. King Ahaz had closed the gates of the temple—Hezekiah not only reopened them, but put the whole building into a time of repair, and revived the use of the psalms of David and Asaph in public worship.

Each person played his or her part in this community-wide honoring of God. They worshiped God through hymns and through reading His Word.

Once they had carried out sacrifices and took their own hearts before the Lord, the assembly was invited to come and bring their personal offerings. One of the great purposes of the temple—as a place for the personal sacrifice and worship of the believer—was now restored.

01 . When you envision the people in your life who are far from God joining you in worship at your church, who comes to mind? Journal a plan to invite them to church this week.

Hezekiah restored the payment of the tithes (ten percent of people's resources) fixed by the Law of Moses, including "the best of the grain, new wine, fresh oil, honey, and of all the produce of the field, and they brought in an abundance, a tenth of everything" (31:5). Without oppressing the people, his wise and upright rule kept his treasury always full, and his palace boasted of stores of spices and costly oil, and plenty of military supplies. Second Kings reflects upon him like this: "Hezekiah relied on the Lord God of Israel; not one of the kings of Judah was like him, either before him or after him" (2 Kings 18:5).

02 . Could your own heart use some Hezekiah-style restoration? If Hezekiah were to revive worship in your own heart, what would he throw out and what would he build?

03 . Journal a prayer to God expressing honestly how you feel about tithing—giving ten percent of what you earn to Him. Commit to God to try tithing this week and make a note of what it does in your heart.

PERSONAL STUDY 03.

(continue studying on your own)

Read 2 Kings 18:9-12; 2 Chron. 30:1-27.

The northern kingdom of Israel had come to ruin. Though there had been animosity between Israel and the people of Judah (the Southern Kingdom) where King Hezekiah reigned, it was gone. Most of the people of Israel had been taken away to Assyria as prisoners, and only a fraction of their former population remained. Messengers from King Hezekiah were sent through the whole land, inviting all to come to the Passover at Jerusalem.

01 . When you graduate from your current level of schooling and move on to the next phase, will you wish that you had defied the crowd and stood more boldly for God? Why, or why not?

Preparations had to be made for such a gathering. Because he was strict in his obedience to the law given through Moses, Hezekiah caused Jerusalem to be thoroughly purified. The idolatrous altars raised by Ahaz were destroyed, and their material was thrown into the Kidron Valley. Enthusiasm began to spread through the whole community.

Priests and Levites who had neglected to complete their ceremonial cleansing were encouraged to do so. As in former times, household fathers and Levites sacrificed the lambs for their families. Perhaps because of the idolatry in their land, many of the visitors from the north failed to comply with the ceremonial demands of the day, but Hezekiah declared they should join in the feast as well. He prayed for them, so that they would not suffer as threatened in Leviticus, for neglect of the commandments of the Law.

02 . Hezekiah's bold stance is inspiring. What would need to change in your heart for you to be willing to lead such a charge in your own ministry, small group, or Christian club at school?

Then came the great celebration and along with it chants, music, sacrifices, and general gladness, as happened in the dedication of the temple by Solomon. Seven days, the legal duration, was not long enough for such a jubilee; the feast was prolonged for seven more days. For two weeks, the people of the Northern and Southern Kingdoms worshiped and celebrated their God, all at the initiation of Hezekiah.

03 . From one to ten, with one being "not at all" and ten being "extremely," how passionate are you about each of the activities that take up your time and energy? Make a list. Be totally honest when you score the passion you have for worship—where does it land?

Hezekiah did all he could to make the revival of worship permanent. In the middle of it all, Isaiah and other prophets were fiercely proclaiming spiritual truth. Many of their messages focused on a vision of the future. The nation began to eagerly anticipate the Messiah: God's deliverer who would restore peace, order, and Israel's place among the nations.

04 . Have you ever found yourself thinking about the return of Christ? What questions do you have?

The LORD heard Hezekiah and

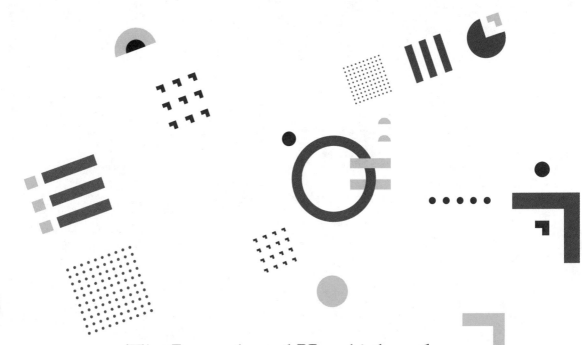

HEALED

the people.

2 Chronicles 30:20

06

introduction

Just how much do the beliefs of older generations impact your beliefs? The story of Josiah is a testimony to the Lord's ability to work in and through those who acknowledge Him as the one true God, even if their parents and grandparents before them did not. Josiah's life is set before us as an example of the transforming impact the choice to follow God can make.

Josiah was born in 648 BC to the family of a young sixteen-year-old Amon, son of Manasseh, king of Judah. Amon was both young and wicked. He died eight years later, after reigning two years as king, and his son Josiah became king at the age of eight. In a land saturated with the influences of idolatry, Josiah stands as one who chose to seek the Lord as David had—to follow the Lord and His Word fully, regardless of what others did. In the Scriptural account of the life of Josiah, we find many others who were willing to follow God in the midst of a society that followed its own desires. We can learn many lessons from the life, times, and choices of Josiah, lessons that will serve us well in a time much like his.

Is there someone you hope that you make proud? Who is it?

Who do you hope will carry on your legacy one day? What do you hope they say about you?

ISRAEL'S GOOD KING
josiah

Before him there was no king like him who turned to the LORD with all his heart and with all his soul and with all his strength according to all the law of Moses, and no one like him arose after him.

2 KINGS 23:25

BEFORE HIM THERE WAS NO KING

GROUP DISCUSSION

(get started)

focus attention

How has the home you are growing up in affected your faith?

**WHO
TURNED TO
THE LORD**

explore the text

AS A GROUP, READ 2 KINGS 21:19-24. ✳︎✎

01 . What is the legacy of Amon, Josiah's father? In other words, how was he remembered?

02 . What might it have been like to grow up as a young boy under such a father? How might Amon's beliefs and choices have impacted young Josiah?

AS A GROUP, READ 2 KINGS 22:1-7. ✳︎✎

03 . It is uncommon for the names of mothers to be mentioned when a king's genealogy is recorded. Why might the author have put Josiah's mother's name in his story?

04 . Notice that this repair project began at the temple. What if it had begun in some other, more practical, part of the kingdom?

If the people of God in a given culture let truth slip away, then their whole society will crumble. Problems in families, problems with money, and problems with enforcing the law indicate spiritual dysfunction. However, when a society experiences revival, other things begin to fall into place.

AS A GROUP, READ 2 KINGS 22:8-13. ✳︎✎

05 . Why did Josiah respond so strongly to what he read in the newly found book of the Law? Was his reaction justified? Explain.

apply the text

Crowned at only eight years old, tiny Josiah would grow to be one of Judah's greatest kings! Certainly he was impacted by the repentance of his grandfather, Manasseh. Another major influence on him was the prophet Zephaniah, whose ministry began a year before Josiah took the throne and continued until he was about seventeen years old. Zephaniah's message of soon-coming judgment from the Lord may have been the catalyst for a turning point in Josiah's life at age sixteen, when we are told that he "began to seek the God of his ancestor David" (2 Chron. 34:3). At twenty-four, he began purging Judah and Jerusalem of idols and improper worship.

06 . What are some of the marks of Josiah's faith that are most meaningful to you?

07 . How could you be a bigger influence in the life of someone who is young in his or her faith?

08 . Who has had the most positive influence on your spiritual life so far? Call or write this person a note to show appreciation for his or her influence on you.

CLOSE YOUR GROUP TIME IN PRAYER, REFLECTING ON WHAT YOU HAVE DISCUSSED. ✳✐

WITH ALL HIS HEART AND SOUL

01. —
02. —
03. —
04. —
05. —

01. —
02. —
03. —

josiah
ISRAEL'S GOOD KING

known for

- Josiah's father inherited the throne at age twenty-two and served two years before being assassinated. His father and grandfather were idolatrous and wicked, contrasting sharply with Josiah's faithfulness to the Lord.

- In the eighteenth year of Josiah's reign, the king ordered the repair of the temple. In the process, the book of the Law was found and read. Josiah initiated a covenant renewal service in the temple (**2 Kings 22:3-13; 23:1-3**).

- Josiah brought changes that included purging the land of idols and pagan altars. He destroyed an altar to the false god Molech where child sacrifice was practiced (**2 Kings 23:4-20**).

- Josiah reinstated the observance of the Passover in Jerusalem, which by some accounts had not been observed in the city for more than four centuries (**2 Kings 23:21-23; 2 Chron. 35:1-19**).

- Josiah's reign ended when he led his army to the Valley of Megiddo against the Egyptian pharaoh's troops (**2 Kings 23:28-30; 2 Chron. 35:20-24**).

basic facts

- Grandson of Manasseh and son of King Amon and Jedidah. He became Judah's fifteenth king.
- Name Josiah means "Yahweh (the Lord) is my healing [or support]."
- Became king of Judah at age eight when his father was assassinated after only two years as ruler.

04 . Had a spiritual experience of renewal at age sixteen that led to radical reforms throughout Judah.

05 . Reigned thirty-one years until his death in battle at Megiddo in 609 BC.

PERSONAL STUDY 01.

(continue studying on your own)
Read 2 Chronicles 34:1-8.

Josiah grew up with a father and grandfather who did not follow God (although his grandfather, Manasseh, did repent and led spiritual reforms that were supposed to draw the nation back to God).

> **01.** Which of your family members has had the greatest positive impact on your spiritual growth and development? Why do you say that?

"In the eighth year of his reign," Josiah would have been sixteen (he became king at age eight). He was still a young man and had not yet undertaken public duties—he probably was under the control and direction of a supervisor. However, he seemed to take God more seriously than his teachers. When he was twenty-one, he led major changes in Judah and Jerusalem, getting rid of various forms of pagan worship: the high places, the Asherah poles, the carved idols, and images of false gods.

Josiah was determined to repair the spiritual damage from the reign of his grandfather, Manasseh. Ultimately, he was unable to free the people of their attachments to paganism (the worship of false gods). It is in this sense that kings rightly attribute the decline and fall of Judah to Manasseh's reign. Neither Josiah nor anyone else was able to pull back the forces Manasseh had released early in his time as king.

Verses 4-5 take up further details of Josiah's reform (compare v. 4b with 2 Kings 23:6; and v. 5a with 2 Kings 23:14,16,20). Though not explicitly stated, it is implied that Josiah executed the priests of Baal (2 Kings 23:20) following the example set by Jehu in 2 Kings 10 and Jehoiada in 2 Chronicles 23:17. The grim punishment was fitted to the crime: the priests who burned sacrifices to Baal had their own bones burned on the same altar. According to 2 Kings 23:16, the bones of priests who had died were removed from their graves and burned.

02 . Why is it important to remove sin and sinful influences from your life? What happens when you let sinful influences linger?

If you take anything short of a Josiah-style approach to those sinful influences that cause you to stumble over and over, it is like inviting sin back into your life. As Christians, we are to count ourselves dead to sin (Rom. 6). So, if something causes you to fall repeatedly, it is better to remove it.

03 . What do you find surprising about the changes Josiah brought about? What would you say to someone who thought Josiah was going too far?

This passage of Scripture shows us several important things. First, Josiah was a very young man, yet he had a spiritual maturity and depth that was not found in his father and grandfather. He was convicted that the right thing to do was follow God and worship Him only. His list of changes to his kingdom is long and extensive indeed. Sin had become so commonplace that it took massive reform to get the people to remove the pagan worship places and practices instituted by Josiah's father and grandfather.

If you've come from a home where Christ was not served and honored, you can be just like Josiah and make a break with that lifestyle that doesn't satisfy. Josiah broke the cycle in his family, and you can too.

PERSONAL STUDY 02.

(continue studying on your own)
Read 2 Chronicles 34:14-21.

In the process of cleaning and repairing the temple, Hilkiah the high priest found a copy of the Book of the Law (2 Chron. 34:14). It might have been hidden by a priest to protect it from destruction at the hands of one of the wicked kings such as Manasseh (Josiah's grandfather) or Amon (Josiah's father). Perhaps it had been removed when the ark was removed from the Holy of Holies by one of these kings.

Hilkiah read the Book of the Law to the king, and Josiah was struck by the seriousness of being in a covenant relationship with the Lord God of Israel. Josiah realized that Judah deserved the wrath of God for their unfaithfulness.

01 . When you observe Josiah's passion for the Word of God and you look honestly at your own heart, what do you see?

Josiah tore his robes in anguish over the evident sin of the people of Judah. His first action was to send his most trusted men to inquire of the Lord for him and for those in Israel and Judah. He wanted to know what the Lord would say at this time in the life of the nation. Josiah knew the absolute necessity of obeying the Word of God, and he was seeking to do that with all his heart.

02 . Read 2 Kings 22:15-17. Why was this going to happen (v. 17)? Confess to God any practices in your own life that fall short of His best for you.

JAMES

AND HE SHALL

HUMBLE YOURSELVES

Humble yourselves
in the sight of the
Lord, and he shall
lift you up.
JAMES 4:10

IN SIGHT OF THE LORD

LIFT YOU UP

4:10

The message was clear: Because they had forsaken the Lord and followed other gods, the Lord's wrath would certainly come upon them. God had warned them, and now He fulfilled His Word. Judah would "become a desolation and a curse" (2 Kings 22:19).

03 . Read 2 Kings 22:18-20. What was God's message to Josiah? When your heart has been tender and humble like Josiah's, what was different in your prayer life?

The message to Josiah was also a fulfillment of the Word of God. Josiah had a tender heart, sensitive to what the Lord said. When he heard the Word, he immediately humbled himself before the Lord. He wept and cried out to the Lord in prayer. Because of that, God allowed Josiah to die in peace without seeing the desolation the Lord would bring on Judah and its inhabitants.

04 . Read 2 Kings 23:1-3. What place did the Word of God take in Josiah's thoughts and actions? The sign of faith in Christ is baptism—do you need to speak your parents and ministry leaders about taking this step in your relationship with God?

The first thing Josiah did was call the elders of Judah and Jerusalem to a meeting at the temple. The people of Judah and Jerusalem went along with him. Josiah had little to say. He simply began reading the words of the book of the covenant, which could have included all the first five Books of the Law. He made a personal covenant to follow the Lord and His Word. The people followed his lead and entered into that covenant. The Word of God made an impact not only on Josiah, but—under his leadership—on the nation as well.

PERSONAL STUDY 03.

(continue studying on your own)
Read 2 Chronicles 35:1-27.

In his eighteenth year as king, Josiah revived the celebration of Passover. Evidently, Passover had not been observed this way since the days of the prophet Samuel (2 Chron. 35:18). King Josiah and his officials worked diligently to make the Passover an important event again, one in which people remembered the past and celebrated God's goodness to them.

Passover was one of Israel's most important celebrations, a commemoration of a significant event: God's deliverance of Israel from slavery to the Egyptians. God's angel passed over every home in which the family had sprinkled blood on its doorpost in obedience to God's command; but when the Lord's angel saw a home with no blood covering the doorpost, the life of the home's firstborn was taken (see Ex. 12:1-30).

Before the Passover could be observed by the people, the leaders of the people had to prepare for the celebration. King Josiah "encouraged them to serve in the Lord's temple" (2 35:2). The religious leaders who served in the temple needed encouragement because the work they were instructed to do would set the tone for the entire Passover celebration. King Josiah encouraged them to return to God's Word, and to make preparations according to the instructions given by Moses and King David.

01 . The Passover meal is what Jesus used to teach us about communion. The next time you take communion, prepare yourself to by praying through God's instructions in 1 Corinthians 11:23-34.

Love God with all your

HEART AND MIND

Mark 12:30

King Josiah and his officials took the lead in providing for the Passover celebration. Josiah reached deep into his own pockets and provided a total of 30,000 sheep and goats for the Passover (2 Chron. 35:7). He also provided three thousand cattle, all from his own possessions. Josiah's officials also joined in by providing generously. Scripture says they gave generously by providing (voluntarily) much of what was needed for the people and for the Levites, the religious leaders who would be overseeing the celebration itself (35:8-9).

02 . Share your heart with God about giving to your church. If you are apprehensive about it, tell God why.

03 . Write a list your most cherished possessions. Then, next to each item, write the words, "Thank you God for this!"

King Josiah is an example of a king who broke with family tradition. Remember that his father and grandfather were evil leaders who did not honor God. Josiah became king at age eight, and in time he broke with his family's tradition of rebelling against God by leading the nation back to God, removing detestable worship practices to false gods, and returning the heart of the people back to God through things like this elaborate and meaningful worship centered around Passover.

Give thanks to God for all that He has provided. Commit to give generously to His mission and pray for your church's unity the next time you observe communion.

TIPS FOR LEADING A SMALL GROUP

Follow these guidelines to prepare for each group session.

// Prayerfully Prepare

REVIEW

Review the weekly material and group questions ahead of time.

PRAY

Be intentional about praying for each person in the group. Ask the Holy Spirit to work through you and the group discussion as you point to Jesus each week through God's Word.

// Minimize Distractions

Create a comfortable environment. If students are uncomfortable, they'll be distracted and therefore not engaged in the group experience. Plan ahead by considering these details:

SEATING

TEMPERATURE

LIGHTING

FOOD OR DRINK

SURROUNDING NOISE

GENERAL CLEANLINESS

At best, thoughtfulness and hospitality show students they're welcome and valued in whatever environment you choose to gather. At worst, people may never notice your effort, but they're also not distracted. Do everything in your ability to help students focus on what's most important: connecting with God, with the Bible, and with one another.

⁄⁄ Include Others

Your goal is to foster a community in which people are welcome just as they are but encouraged to grow spiritually. Always be aware of opportunities to include any students who visit the group and encourage group members to invite their friends. An inexpensive way to make first-time guests feel welcome or to invite someone to get involved is to give them their own copies of this Bible study book.

⁄⁄ Encourage Discussion

A good small-group experience has the following characteristics.

EVERYONE PARTICIPATES

Encourage everyone to ask questions, share responses, or read aloud. Since some students may not read as well as others, don't call on students to read out loud— ask for volunteers.

NO ONE DOMINATES—NOT EVEN THE LEADER

Be sure that your time speaking as a leader takes up less than half of your time together as a group. Politely guide discussion if anyone dominates.

NOBODY IS RUSHED THROUGH QUESTIONS

Don't feel that a moment of silence is a bad thing. People often need time to think about their responses to questions they've just heard or to gain courage to share what God is stirring in their hearts.

INPUT IS AFFIRMED AND FOLLOWED UP

Make sure you point out something true or helpful in a response. Don't just move on. Build community with follow-up questions, asking how other people have experienced similar things or how a truth has shaped their understanding of God and the Scripture you're studying. Students will be less likely to speak up if they fear that you don't actually want to hear their answers or that you're looking for only a certain answer.

GOD AND HIS WORD ARE CENTRAL

Opinions and experiences can be helpful, but God has given us the truth. Trust God's Word to be the authority and God's Spirit to work in people's lives. You can't change anyone, but God can. Continually point students to the Word and to active steps of faith.

HOW TO USE THE LEADER GUIDE

Prepare to Lead

Each session of the Leader Guide is designed to be torn out so you, the leader, can have this front-and-back page with you as you lead your group through the session.

Focus Attention

These questions are provided to help get the discussion started. They are generally more introductory and topical in nature.

Explore the Text

Questions in this section have some sample answers or discussion prompts provided in the Leader Guide, if needed, to help you jump-start or steer the conversation.

Apply the Text

This section contains questions that allow group members an opportunity to apply the content they have been discussing together.

Biography

This section isn't covered in the Leader Guide and may be used during the group session or by group members as a part of the personal study time during the week. If you choose to use them during your group session, make sure you are familiar with the content and how you intend to use it before your group meets.

leader guide
session 1

Focus Attention

Do you think of yourself as a detail-oriented person? Why is it important to pay attention to details even though it might not come naturally to us?

- Sometimes details are super important—miss one the enter project you are working on could go wrong. Similarly, in today's text King Saul ignored crucial details in God's instructions to him.

Explore The Text

ASK A VOLUNTEER TO READ 1 SAMUEL 13:1,5-14. ✳

01. In what specific ways did Saul disobey God in these verses, and why was his disobedience so serious? In what ways can fear prompt people to disobey God?

- Saul made the burnt offering (not his role or place to do so) instead of waiting on the prophet Samuel to arrive and perform the function.

- Fear can cause people to be paralyzed to the point that they choose not to act on something they know God has commanded them to do.

02. Was Saul's punishment too severe? Why or why not?

- Partial obedience is complete disobedience and Saul's disobedience was rampant.

ASK A VOLUNTEER TO READ 1 SAMUEL 15:1-3.

03. Why did the Amalekites deserve such a severe punishment? Does the shocking nature of this text make it untrue?

- As He did in the flood, God has exercised judgment upon entire societies. He does this after extensive warnings and always provides deliverance even in the midst of His wrath.

- Having negative feelings against God's Word does not make it untrue.

04 . Yet again, Saul and his army only partially complied with the Lord's command. Why did they disobey this time? What was the Lord's reaction to this?

- Saul followed God's command to slay the Amalekites, but he did not obey completely.

- Israel kept the best of the plunder—the good things—and destroyed the weak or despised things they found.

05 . Saul built a monument to himself. Based on this, what did he think about himself, and what did he think about God?

- Instead of glorifying God, Saul glorified himself. This amounts to self-worship: holding himself in higher esteem than he held God.

06 . Do you think Saul was truly surprised that his behaviors were sinful, or do you think he was attempting to make his disobedience seem more acceptable? Explain.

- Saul failed to realize that what pleases the Lord is obedience, not the religious rituals themselves.

Apply The Text

While we may not hear the words of God audibly from the prophet Samuel, we are reading Samuel's words in the Bible. Like Saul, we have heard directly from God and, in our New Testament setting, can see His will in His Word. Before coming down too hard on Saul, let us consider times we have done the same things. Through social media, we might build monuments to ourselves. Through compromising with sin, we might be guilty of the same kind of disobedience. As we look to Saul, we sometimes see our own reflections. What's the main point of the story—what Elijah did for God or what God did through Elijah? Why does it matter that we understand the difference?

07 . Why is partial obedience to God insufficient? What is necessary instead?

08 . Inspired by the way Samuel guided Saul, what are some simple ways we as a group can encourage one another in the coming week?

09 . "To obey is better than sacrifice" (1 Sam. 15:22). In what areas are you substituting sacrifice for obedience?

leader guide
session 2

Focus Attention

List some qualities people look for in a person who is going to lead a nation. What is the most important quality in your opinion?

- People differ on what they consider to be important qualities. Charisma, wealth, success, military training, or experience in politics are frequently prized characteristics. However, the leadership qualities that are important to God are completely different from ours.

Explore The Text

ASK A VOLUNTEER TO READ 1 SAMUEL 16:1-10.

01. Why did Samuel initially think Eliab was the Lord's choice? What's the twist here (see 1 Sam. 10:23-24)?

- Given Eliab's stature—that is, his physical appearance—Samuel initially believed him to be the one God had chosen. Ironically, Samuel was drawn to someone who resembled the physical characteristics of Saul, and the Lord used this experience to teach Samuel something important.

02. What does verse 7 suggest about the qualities God counts as most important for His servants?

- Our culture evaluates people by their appearance, social status, and other superficial traits. Nevertheless, people do not see what God sees. Outward appearances often deceive people, but they never deceive God.

ASK VOLUNTEER TO READ 1 SAMUEL 16:11-13.

03. What characteristic would seem to hinder David from being anointed as king (v. 11)?

- Jesse's assumption was that David was disqualified from consideration due to his young age, which is why he was not even present for Samuel.

04 . What did David's faithfulness in watching the sheep say about his character? How did this prepare him for his future (see 1 Sam. 17:34-37; Ps. 23)?

- God had been working behind the scenes in David's life in order to prepare him for his future role as king. Tending sheep helped prepare David to rule Israel. God intended for the king to care for people with the same compassion that a shepherd gives to the flock.

Apply The Text

Throughout the Bible, God chose unlikely people to join Him in His plans to redeem humanity from sin. You may not think of yourself as a likely candidate to lead others spiritually in any way, but the Bible is full of people with less than perfect backgrounds. It seems that these are the kinds of people God chooses— broken and imperfect, yet full of promise when they seek forgiveness, strive to do God's will, repent of past mistakes, and move on in the grace only God can provide.

05 . Who do you identify with most in this story: Samuel, Jesse, Jesse's sons, or David? Why?

06 . How might knowing that God has chosen you to serve Him change the way that you view your place in this world?

leader guide
session 3

Focus Attention

What is the number one source people turn to for wisdom today? What happens when our source of wisdom is flawed?

- Behind all helpful forms of technology that answer questions, we find people who are imperfect just like us. If the foundation of our wisdom is flawed, we will make flawed decisions.

Explore The Text

ASK A VOLUNTEER TO READ 1 KINGS 3:1-9.

01. How would you respond if God offered to give you anything you asked? Why?

- God saw Solomon's heart to serve and worship Him, and He asked Solomon to name a gift that he wanted to receive from the Lord.

02. Why did Solomon desire wisdom above anything else? What does this reveal about him and his relationship with God?

- Solomon acknowledged that God was the cause of his rise to power. Though he lacked experience, he had to lead God's chosen people and needed to embody God's standards for them. With all of the growth in their numbers under his father David, Solomon likely sensed that the old ways of governing would not meet the current needs of his subjects. Given this personal dilemma, Solomon requested a discerning heart, or wisdom, revealing his attitude toward the Lord of humility.

03. What situation in your life right now makes you feel inadequate? What difference has God's wisdom made in how you have (or have not) dealt with that situation?

ASK A VOLUNTEER TO READ 1 KINGS 3:10-15.

04 . What does God's willingness to give Solomon more than he asked for reveal about His nature? How have you witnessed God's generosity in your own life?

- God's willingness to give Solomon more than he requested demonstrates the generous and benevolent nature of God. He is a good God who loves to bless His people.

Apply The Text

Even though Solomon did not ask for riches, God gave him riches along with wisdom. God does not promise to give you wealth, but He does promise to meet all your needs. God wants you to put Him first in your life, to fill your mind with His desires, to imitate Him, and to serve and obey Him in everything. Then He will give you what you need from day to day.

05 . In what ways do you value living with godly wisdom more than pursuing wealth or achievements?

06 . What are some blessings that might accompany God-given wisdom, and how might you use those blessings in God's service?

leader guide
session 4

Focus Attention

Have you ever felt the need to make a clean break with your past? Explain.

Explore The Text

ASK A VOLUNTEER TO READ 2 CHRONICLES 14:1-5.

01 . What is Asa's overall legacy? How did Asa's faithfulness impact the everyday lives of the people?

- Broadly speaking, Asa was a theologically sound leader who acted in accordance with his beliefs. Asa destroyed the illegitimate cult objects— altars, high places, the standing stones representing Baal, and the Asherah poles, wooden poles representing the goddess Asherah. As a result, the people experienced a significant degree of peace and prosperity.

02 . Note the phrase "seek the Lord" in verse 4. What does it look like, in basic terms, for people to seek the Lord? What happens to societies that seek the Lord?

- For those in Asa's day, the phrase "seek the Lord" described how one was to respond to God. It involved more than a specific act of seeking God's help and guidance—it stood for one's whole duty toward God. In other words, it is knowing God and being wholeheartedly devoted to Him. In Asa's time, this meant repentance from idol worship and the destruction of all that might have been a representation of that worship.

03 . What forms of idol worship are prevalent in our culture today? What is appealing about them?

- At its root meaning, idolatry is the worship of created things in place of the worship of Creator God. We live in an age of distraction. We are pulled in many different directions by technology, social media, friends, work, and hobbies. These can be very good things, but they can also easily distract us from what is most important. God created us to love, worship, and enjoy Him. When we elevate anything to (or above!) the place of God, that thing becomes an idol.

04 . Why do you think we so easily fall into the trap of giving our hearts to idols? What are some of the excuses we use for worshiping idols?

- Nothing outside of God can truly satisfy our souls. We are tempted to believe that lesser things will bring lasting satisfaction or enjoyment, even though experience tells us otherwise. Only through the person and work of Jesus Christ can we find true fulfillment and satisfaction. All other objects of worship will ultimately fail us.

Apply The Text

The "good and right" that Asa did was to remove the foreign (Canaanite) altars, high places, sacred pillars, and the Asherim. Not only did he remove the negative influences of Baal worship, but Asa also commanded Judah to seek the Lord and study His Word (the Law). As a result of Asa's "clean-up" campaign, the land was undisturbed for ten years, and, instead of putting their energies into war, they were able to strengthen and grow the nation. God had redefined Asa's family legacy.

05 . Have you allowed your family background to keep you from serving the Lord? How might you make a break with the past and serve the Lord today?

06 . Idolatry is the worship of something created rather than the Creator. What man-made things come between you and God?

07 . What would our life look like if we truly chose to worship God above everything else? How would this look different than how you live life now?

Focus Attention

What causes Christians to give up hope? Why do we sometimes focus more on discouragement than on the truth?

- Satan cannot revoke the gospel, but he can cause Christians to forget it for a moment. Then, when they are singled out from the crowd, Christians can feel isolated and discouraged. Fortunately, the gospel is just as true when we feel alone in our faith.

Explore The Text

ASK A VOLUNTEER TO READ 2 KINGS 18:28-32.

01. Suppose you were a Hebrew standing on the wall. How would you feel after hearing Rabshakeh's words?

- A Hebrew hearing these words probably felt terror as they thought about being conquered by a foreign power. A Hebrew standing on Jerusalem's wall might also have felt abandoned by God, wondering why He was allowing a nation that worshiped untrue gods to threaten His people in their capital.

02. Have you encountered a "Rabshakeh," someone who has tried to discourage you and tempt you to give up your trust in the Lord, claiming it was in order to rescue you? How did you respond?

- We need to make peace with those who do not support our beliefs and who try to discourage us. Follow what you know to be true and do not let anyone come in the way. Whether people support you or not, you don't want to look back in regret one day because you missed what God had for you.

ASK A VOLUNTEER TO READ 2 KINGS 19:1-7.

03. What was Hezekiah's first response when he heard what Rabshakeh had said (vv. 1-2)? What did this response say about his character and relationship with the Lord?

- To tear one's clothes and put on itchy sackcloth was an outward sign of intense grief in one's heart. According to verse 37 of the previous chapter, the court secretary, the court historian, and the man in charge of the palace had all torn their clothes as well. Hezekiah's hope (v. 4) was that the Lord would hear what was said about Him and rebuke the one who said it.

04 . What did Hezekiah do with the threatening letter from Sennacherib? Why did he do this?

- Hezekiah read the letter, spread the letter out before the Lord in the temple, and then prayed to the God of heaven. Hezekiah placed the letter on the floor and brought the threat to the Lord, recognizing that God was the only One mighty enough to help.

05 . What reason did Hezekiah give for God to save His people? How should this impact your own prayers?

- Hezekiah prayed for God to save his people in order for the fame of the Lord to spread to other peoples on earth. Hezekiah wanted others to know that there is only one true God who is worthy of honor and glory.

Apply The Text

The psalmist affirms, "The Lord has heard my plea for help; the Lord accepts my prayer" (Ps. 6:9). The Lord can accomplish infinitely more than we would ever dare to ask or hope. His mighty power is at work within us. What an incredible thought! The God who created the universe loves us. He cares for us. He fights our battles while we keep silent. Nothing is impossible for Him. Whatever seemingly hopeless situation we find ourselves in, God can rescue us. May He be who we turn to first in such moments, not last.

06 . What is one situation in your life that has seemed so hopeless that you have stopped praying about it?

07 . What are some specific ways the story of Hezekiah should influence your prayer life?

08 . How can our group support you in prayer this week?

leader guide
session 6

Focus Attention

How has the home you are growing up in affected your faith?

- It is a blessing to grow up in a family with generations of spiritual faithfulness to uphold you, but being the first Christian in your family is another blessing altogether!

Explore The Text

ASK A VOLUNTEER TO READ 2 KINGS 21:19-24.

01. What is the legacy Amon, Josiah's father? How was he remembered?

- Amon walked in the old idol-worshiping ways of his father Manasseh, sacrificing to the carved images in the land. He did not follow in Manasseh's call to serve only the Lord of Israel. Instead, he walked in pride and did much evil in the sight of the Lord, multiplying his sin and guilt. His palace servants conspired to kill him, and Amon's two-year reign ended at their hands. The people of the land executed those responsible for Amon's death and placed Josiah as king over Judah.

02. What might it have been like to grow up as a young boy under such a father? How might Amon's beliefs and choices have impacted young Josiah?

ASK A VOLUNTEER TO READ 2 KINGS 22:1-7.

03. It is uncommon for the names of mothers to be mentioned when a king's genealogy is recorded. Why might the author have put Josiah's mother's name in his story?

- One probable reason for mentioning Josiah's mother would be to at least subtly imply that many of the positive traits the reader would see in Josiah were at least partially due to her influence.

04. Notice that this repair project began at the temple. What if it had begun in some other, more practical, part of the kingdom?

- If the people of God in a given culture let truth slip away, then their whole society will crumble. Problems in families, problems with money, and problems with enforcing the law indicate spiritual decline. However, when a society experiences revival, other things begin to fall into place.

ASK A VOLUNTEER TO READ 2 KINGS 22:8-13.

05 . Why did Josiah respond so strongly to what he read in the newly found Book of the Law? Was his reaction justified? Explain.

- Scripture influenced Josiah's actions greatly. Moses' writings were not obeyed through the centuries, but Josiah's personal commitment grew when he determined that God spoke to Moses and made a covenant with Israel. Josiah acted with the confidence that he was doing God's will, based on God's Word, in service to God's people. Josiah tore his garment when he heard God's Law, and sought a prophetic word to interpret the consequences of his and his people's disobedience. He admitted the nation's sin, feared its results, and hoped it was not too late to change. He seemed to reason that God could act mercifully toward an undeserving people.

Apply The Text

Crowned at only eight years old, tiny Josiah would grow to be one of Judah's greatest kings! Certainly he was impacted by the repentance of his grandfather, Manasseh. Another major influence was the prophet Zephaniah, whose ministry began a year before Josiah took the throne and continued until he was about seventeen years old. Zephaniah's message of soon-coming judgment from the Lord may have been the catalyst for a turning point in Josiah at age sixteen, when we are told that he "began to seek the God of his ancestor David" (2 Chron. 34:3). At twenty-four, he began removing idols from Judah and Jerusalem and encouraging right worship of the Lord.

06 . What are some of the marks of Josiah's faith that are most meaningful to you?

07 . How could you be a bigger influence in the life of someone who is young in his or her faith?

08 . Who has had the most positive influence on your spiritual life so far? Call or write this person a note to show appreciation for his or her influence on you.

notes

notes

notes

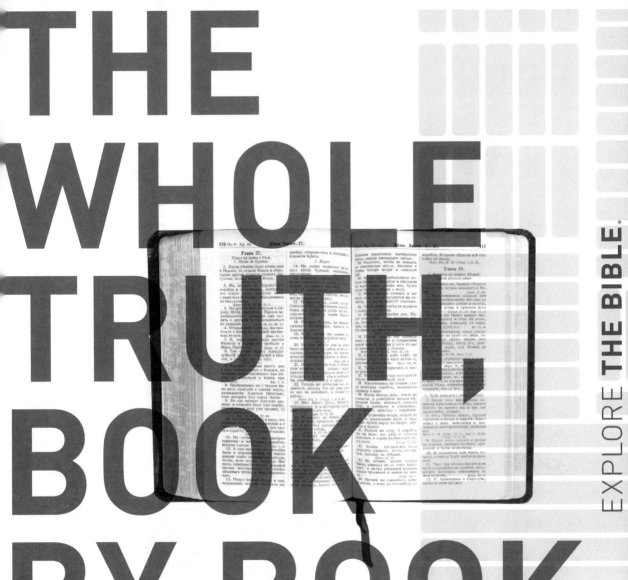

THE WHOLE TRUTH, BOOK BY BOOK

When you Explore the Bible book by book, you give students the whole truth of God's Word. Each Bible study session frames Scripture with biblical and historical context vital to understanding its original intent, and unpacks the transforming truth of God in a manner that is practical, age-appropriate, and repeatable over a lifetime.

Download a free sample at
goexplorethebible.com/students

EXPLORE **THE BIBLE**
FOR STUDENTS

WHERE TO GO
FROM HERE

We hope you've enjoyed learning about the characters of the Bible, but you've only just begun! Don't miss *Characters Volume 4: The Prophets* where we unpack the grace of God in the lives of those who proclaimed His message—prophets like Isaiah, Jeremiah, Jonah, and Ezekiel. These people proclaimed God's message of hope and looked forward to Jesus.

For more information, call 800.458.2772 or visit: lifeway.com